Doily tatted in DMC 100 crochet thread by Linda Williams, from a mid twentieth-century pattern published by the American Thread Company.

TATTING
Pam Palme

Shire Publications Ltd

CONTENTS

Introduction 3

Knotting 5

Early techniques, tools and design 10

Tatting in Ireland 21

1900 to 1945 22

Modern developments 26

Directions for tatting 30

Further reading 32

Places to visit 32

Published in 1996 by Shire Publications Ltd, Cromwell House, Church Street, Princes Risborough, Buckinghamshire HP27 9AA, UK. Copyright © 1996 by Pam Palmer. First published 1996. Shire Album 323. ISBN 0 7478 0312 9.

Pam Palmer is hereby identified as the author of this work in accordance with Section 77 of the Copyright, Designs and Patents Act 1988.

Printed in Great Britain by CIT Printing Services, Press Buildings, Merlins Bridge, Haverfordwest, Dyfed SA61 1XF.

British Library Cataloguing in Publication Data. Palmer, Pam. Tatting. – (Shire Album; 323). 1. Tatting 2. Lace and lace making I. Title 746. 4'36 ISBN 0-7478-0312-9

ACKNOWLEDGEMENTS

I would like to thank all those who have so generously shared their knowledge, and who have allowed their items to be used as illustrations. Special thanks to my husband, and to Heather Lickley, Enid Riley and Christine Springett for their help and encouragement, to David Springett and Peter Whitwell for taking many of the photographs and to Beverley Florence for typing the manuscript. The extract from *An Elementary Course in Tatting* is reproduced with the kind permission of Coats Patons Crafts.

Illustrations are acknowledged as follows: Trustees of the Victoria and Albert Museum, pages 5, 21; the Embroiderers' Guild Collection, page 6; the Burghley House Collection, page 8 (top); the Wolverhampton Art Gallery Collection, page 8 (bottom); the Marquess of Bath, Longleat House, Warminster, page 9 (bottom); Trustees of the Rachel B. Kay-Shuttleworth Collections, Gawthorpe Hall, pages 11 (top), 20 (top), 22; Luton Museum Service, page 14 (bottom); Coats Patons Crafts, page 27 (top).

Cover: Nineteenth-century collar. (Centre) Bone shuttle with edging. (Bottom) Four Mauchline-ware shuttles (floral decoration, robin transfer 'A Happy Xmas', Stuart tartan, seaweed), carved ivory (Chinese).

Nineteenth-century cuff.

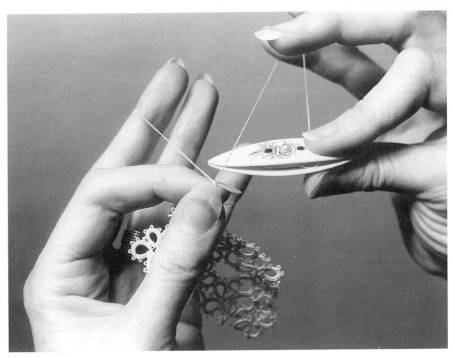

Tatting. The word describes the process and the product. The shuttle is approximately 2¹/₂ inches (65 mm) long. The thread is wound round the post or spool between the two blades. The ends of the shuttle are close enough to prevent the thread unwinding if dropped. The audible click as the ends spring together when the shuttle is wound or unwound is a characteristic of the craft.

INTRODUCTION

Tatting is a knotted lace made in the hand with a small shuttle. Much of the fascination of making it lies in the skilful interplay of fingers, thread and shuttle. It is the fingers which actually form the knot, the shuttle serving only as a convenient device for carrying the thread. The shuttle thread which appears to form the knot becomes the running or foundation thread. This transfer of the knot from one thread to another is central to the craft. All tatting is based on the two movements which form the knot, known as a double stitch. Small loops of thread, called picots, between some of the stitches contribute to its delicate appearance. Tatting can be distinguished from other laces by its char-

acteristic construction of rings and scallop-shaped chains. It is sewn on to fabric as an edging, inset or appliqué. Larger pieces are formed by repeating motifs or working in

The double stitch.

rows or rounds. The uses to which tatting has been put, as a decorative trimming or as a textile in its own right, have reflected contemporary furnishings and fashion.

3

(From top) A partly worked ring. A row of rings. A row of rings and chains. The shuttles are 1990s plastic. The bottom shuttle has a removable spool for easy winding, and an integral hook which dispenses with the need for a separate crochet hook for making joins. (Lower left) 'The Star' motif from a 1934 Weldon's pattern book illustrates design construction: the five centre rings are worked first, followed by a round of ten rings and linking chains; the final outer edge has only chains.

In its present form tatting dates from the mid nineteenth century, when it was considered a genteel accomplishment and pastime for a lady. Mrs Pullan in *Treasures in Needlework* (1855) described it as showing a pretty hand to advantage. It was often thought to be a difficult lace to learn, and *The Dictionary of Needlework* (Caulfeild and Saward, *c*.1880) admitted that, at first, the fingers seemed to be always in the way.

Tatting spread from Europe to the colonies and beyond, taken by early settlers and missionaries. In Margaret Mitchell's novel *Gone with the Wind*, which is set during the American Civil War, Scarlett O'Hara helped to raise funds for a hospital bazaar by tatting yards of lace.

For much of the twentieth century tatting has been less familiar than many other needlecrafts. Basic skills were passed on but some of the early techniques forgotten. The few good examples in museums are often in reserve collections and not on display. References may confuse tatting with knotting, netting or crochet, and shuttles may be erroneously labelled. A combination of these factors has led to a general lack of knowledge about the craft of tatting, its history and potential.

In popular tradition tatting is seen as a 'poor man's lace', in period drama more likely to be worn by the maid than the mistress. Rachel Kay-Shuttleworth, whose collection at Gawthorpe Hall includes some fine pieces, wrote: 'Using the traditional motifs of lozenges, rings, loops and picots, rosettes, semi-rosettes, trefoils and festoons, much variety can be achieved...though much is of course repetitive. This repetition is part of the charm of tatting.'

4

One of a set of late seventeenth-century chairs at Ham House (National Trust), with dark red couched knotting in a formal design on yellow silk.

KNOTTING

Knotting, to prevent the fraying of woven cloth or as applied decoration, was one of man's earliest textile techniques. Knotting thread by hand or by needle was known in Britain in late medieval times, but its popularity in the late seventeenth and eighteenth centuries owes more to eastern tradition. It was a time when trade was expanding and merchants returning from India and the Far East brought with them textiles which influenced European style. Much Chinese embroidery was skilfully worked in Pekin knots, which resemble French knots, in rows for outlines and massed together for fillings. It was a short step to knotting a length of thread by hand and sewing it in place in imitation of embroidered knots. If the unknotted

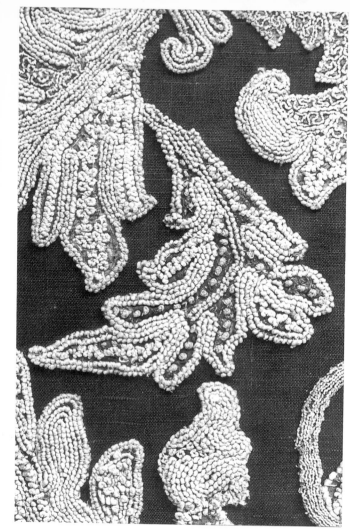

Detail of a mid eight-eenth-century panel, from the Embroiderers' Guild Collection: ecru knotted threads with some surface stitchery on dark brown linen. The work is attributed to Princess Amelia, daughter of George II, and to the Duchess of Newasch; fragments were repaired and remounted by Ruth, Countess of Chichester, in 1955-9.

thread were first wound on to a shuttle a considerable length could be worked. The closely knotted thread was looped into a decorative fringe or couched on fabric in elaborate patterns to which embroidery was added to create a highly textured surface. The patterns often reflected eastern design.

In an article published in 1926 in *The Embroideress*, Louisa Pesel described the technique: 'The actual knotting soon becomes automatic. With the right hand pass the thread through the twisted loop lying over the left fingers, carefully guide the knot into the required place with the first finger and thumb of the left hand, the little finger of that hand gradually pulls the unknotted portion of the thread away from the knot and at the same time tightens the knot. Try it; it is very easy.'

Knotting became a fashionable textile decoration, mostly on household furnishings. A set of chairs at Ham House, Richmond, Surrey, is upholstered in yellow silk with red knotting in a formal design. The brilliance of the original colours can be seen in an unused piece of the same silk and decoration at the Victoria and

Albert Museum. Another length of furnishing fabric, also in the Victoria and Albert Museum, resembles Jacobean crewel work with large flowers and leaves in a free-flowing design. The threads are a mix of silk and cotton on a natural cream background. Petals and leaves are filled with tightly packed rows of knotted thread. Up to four shades of one colour in a petal give a rich linear shaded effect. Further tones are created by using a contrasting colour for the couching thread. Knotting was also often worked in monochrome, such as cream thread on a natural linen fabric. The Victoria and Albert Museum has four small balls of closely knotted silk thread in cream, brown, pale and bright green.

A graceful occupation which required little concentration, knotting became a popular pastime in fashionable society. A number of portraits were painted of ladies knotting, including one of the Countess of Albermarle by Sir Joshua Reynolds in 1759, now in the National Gallery, London. The shuttle and thread provided an elegant pose for the hands. The shuttle was as much a fashion accessory as a needlework tool. Exquisitely made in gold and silver, mother-of-pearl, tortoiseshell and ivory, and decorated with enamel, inlay and jewels, they were regarded as highly acceptable gifts and a source of pride to their owners. They were usually 4 to 6 inches (100 to 150 mm) long; space between the ends allowed the shuttles to be wound with heavy silk or linen thread. French shuttles were generally larger and more ornate than English shuttles. Madame de Pompadour was known to have owned several, including one with cornelian stones set as a bunch of cherries in enamelled gold. Shuttles were made by leading craftsmen of the day. A large tortoiseshell shuttle offered for sale in the 1980s was decorated with tiny flowers and delicate motifs of garden implements and musical instruments inlaid in gold and silver. A surviving papier-mâché shuttle has 'H. CLAY PATENT' impressed on the centre block. Henry Clay was a papier-mâché manufacturer whose commissions for the aristocracy are well documented. The shuttle is 5 inches (127 mm) long and painted black with a border of leaves and fifteen tiny feathers in browns and blues on each side.

Taken to social gatherings or the thea-

Tortoiseshell knotting shuttles. The larger shuttle has decorative gold inlay and is 5 inches (127 mm) long. The smaller shuttle is wound with thread and has a short length of closely worked knotting. The blades of both shuttles are approximately half an inch (13 mm) apart.

Lucy, Duchess of Montrose, by Benjamin Vandergucht (1793), after Andrea Soldi c.1740, at Burghley House, Stamford. The Duchess holds a large shuttle wound with white or cream thread. On her lap is a blue silk knotting bag embroidered with silver. An unusual feature is the winder on which the knotted thread has been wound.

In this charming portrait of Mrs Pearce by Francis Wheatley (1786) in the Wolverhampton Art Gallery, the thread is wound round the fingers of her left hand and the knotted thread can be seen to the right. Her shuttle appears to be little bigger than a tatting shuttle although the ends are clearly apart. The ribbons of her white silk knotting bag, which is delicately embroidered with coloured flowers, hang elegantly over her left wrist.

Knotting shuttle decorated on both sides with insects in stained ivory, tortoiseshell, pearl and amber.

tre, the shuttle and thread would be carried in a silk bag, which itself might be elegantly embroidered. Newspapers carried advertisements offering rewards for shuttles which had been lost or mislaid.

The letters of Mary Delany (1700-88) reveal much about knotting. She described knotting a silk fringe to decorate a knotting bag to contain the gold shuttle given to her by George III. Among the furnishings she made for her home near Dublin were blue linen chair covers with leaves worked in a variety of knotting techniques.

There are a number of contemporary literary references to knotting. Satirical verses by Sir Charles Sedley allude to the Protestant Queen Mary knotting threads when travelling by coach, in contrast to Catholic queens telling beads. A popular song of the time, also by Sedley, told of a suitor ignored as 'Phyllis without frown or smile sat and knotted all the while'. Dr Johnson confessed that 'Dempster's sister' had once tried to teach him to knot but that he had made no progress.

By the end of the eighteenth century the fashion for knotting had declined, partly owing to the increased use of lightweight fabrics which were less suitable for heavy textured trimming.

An eighteenth-century conversation piece: a lady knots while her companion reads. The silhouette, at Longleat House, was painted by Mrs Delany (1700-88).

9

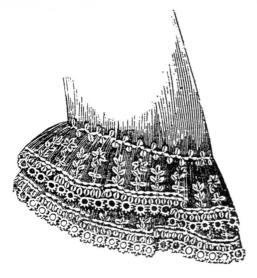

Sleeve trimming from 'The Ladies' Companion' (October 1851). The main design is of cord appliquéd on net, but both frills are edged with a row of tatted rings linked by a short length of unworked thread but not joined at the picots. This is an early use of a very simple edging.

EARLY TECHNIQUES, TOOLS AND DESIGN

Tatting developed naturally and gradually from knotting. This makes it difficult to date, but it is reasonable to assume that a simple form of tatting was being practised by the beginning of the nineteenth century.

Using a technique similar to knotting, but with fine thread and a small shuttle, a series of knots worked over a loop of thread was pulled up into a ring. With the addition of picots, a succession of rings resembled a daisy chain, which was then sewn into a circle. One or two more rows could be sewn around the first, the picots helping to hide the sewing. Needle and thread were also used to work needlelace centres, usually of detached buttonhole stitch. Finally, a number of rosettes were tacked on to a paper pattern and tied together through adjoining picots, creating the lace formation typical of early tatting.

In spite of the limitations imposed by the technique, considerable ingenuity was used to create designs by altering the size and number of the rings,

Handkerchief with a wide border. The design is typical of early tatting. The circular motifs are tatted separately. The tiny knots which tie them together can be clearly seen. The centres are worked with a needle.

Above: *Short baby robe decorated with fine tatting, from the Rachel B. Kay-Shuttleworth Collections (1830-40).*

Right: *Detail from an early collar. An ingenious arrangement of rings creates an attractive inner edge.*

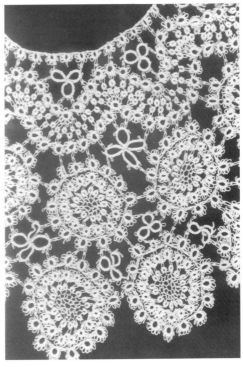

varying the needlelace centres and the shape and size of the motifs. It was obvious, however, that the use of a single thread restricted design, and the need to sew and tie was tedious and time-consuming.

Very basic instructions appeared in 1843 in an anonymous booklet, *The Ladies' Handbook of Millinery, Dressmaking and Tatting*, but the development of the craft was largely due to Mademoiselle Eleonore Riego de la Branchardière, generally known as Mlle Riego. A talented needlewoman and writer, she was the acknowledged authority of her day on crochet, lacework and tatting. Of the hundred or so books she wrote between 1846 and 1887 eleven were on tatting. It was said of her books that no lady's worktable was complete without them. In *Tatting* (1850) Mlle Riego replaced the shuttle with a netting needle. The thread was wound on to the needle, which had an

11

Mlle Eleonore Riego de la Branchardière was born in England. Her mother was Irish and her father came from a noble French family but left France at the time of the Revolution. As well as being a prolific author, Mlle Riego had a needlework establishment in London which sold embroidery and lacemaking supplies.

open eye or fork at each end, and manipulated in the same way as with a shuttle, except that the needle was fine enough to be taken through the picots to effect joins. In the same book she began circular motifs with a centre ring containing a number of picots to which a round of rings was joined, replacing the line of rings sewn into a circle. The centre ring also dispensed with the need for a needlelace filling.

A year later, a method of joining picots without the use of a sewing or netting needle appeared in a small booklet, *Tatting Made Easy*, by an anonymous author known only as 'a Lady'. The picot was placed over the loop making the ring, part of the loop was pulled through the picot with a crochet hook, and the shuttle was taken through the loop. Picots are still

joined in this way. Mlle Riego adopted this method and made no further reference to the netting needle. Its use did not die out immediately, however, for a 'Maltese Insertion in Tatting' in *The Ladies' Book of the Month* (1867) lists 'a fine netting needle' and not a shuttle. The method is now obsolete, but its effect can be imagined from a description in *Gone with the Wind*, when Melanie drove the needle back and forth 'as though handling a rapier in a duel'.

In spite of the technical improvements, designs formed solely of rings had obvious limitations. The ability to work a straight or curved line would considerably increase design potential. Some early patterns gave instructions for using a needle and thread to overcast or buttonhole

Left: *Two edgings. Both are over a yard (metre) long. The lower edge with needle-joined picots and tied motifs is likely to date from the 1840s. The top edge has shuttle-worked joins and would not have been made before 1851.*

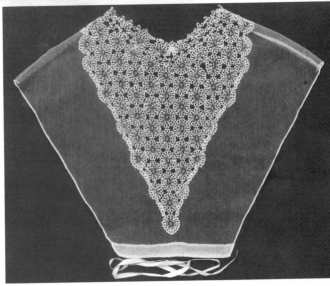

Right: *Chemisette: tatted inset mounted on net. The motifs are formed of two rows of partly closed rings with needle-worked spiders.*

stitch over the unworked thread between rings, creating what would now be called a false chain, but it was not until 1864, in Mlle Riego's *The Royal Tatting Book*, that a true chain was used. It appeared only in a narrow edging but the instructions clearly indicated the use of a second thread forming true tatting stitches. Instead of a loop round the hand forming a ring, the second thread was taken over the back of the hand and both threads were used to work a chain. The term 'chain' is more recent, replacing the earlier 'straight thread', although neither accurately de-

scribes the scalloped lines between rings which are a characteristic feature of tatting. Mlle Riego is usually attributed with the invention of the chain. It was with some justification that she wrote in *The Complete Book of Tatting* (1866): 'I am pleased to find that instead of its being considered a trifling and rather useless amusement it has now become a standard branch of needlework.'

Tatting was included in the major needlework books of the late nineteenth century. Mrs Beeton's *Book of Needlework* (1870), completed and published after her

death, contained a well-illustrated chapter of some eighty pages and included a variety of designs and suggestions for their use. *The Dictionary of Needlework* (c.1880) by Caulfeild and Saward had a comprehensive review of tatting, although the patterns were not new and included some from Mrs Beeton's book. In 1886 Thérèse de Dillmont published her *Encyclopedia of Needlework*. She consolidated and built on techniques and structures already well-established, making frequent use of two shuttles and coloured threads. She is often credited with the introduction of the Josephine picot, a small decorative ring using only half stitches. This was a knotting technique, but it was Mlle Dillmont who named it, it is assumed, in honour of the Empress Josephine.

Tatting shuttles most commonly used were of bone, ivory, mother-of-pearl and tortoiseshell. *The Ladies' Companion* (1851) described a steel shuttle made by the needle manufacturers Boulton & Son as 'more convenient for fine tatting than the old fashioned ivory shuttle which it will doubtless in a great measure supersede'. Mrs Beeton mentioned shuttles of tortoiseshell inlaid with pearl and silver. A Weldon's booklet of the 1880s described tortoiseshell as having 'the desirable quality of extreme lightness'.

With the advent of the railways, middle-class families were able to travel more extensively. This led to the development of the tourist industry and a demand for souvenirs. Centred around the small town of

Handkerchief from the Luton Museum. The design includes chains which date it no earlier than 1864.

14

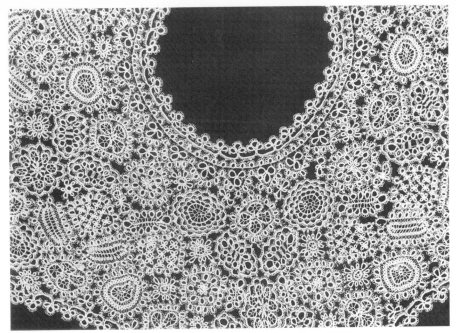

Detail from a large collar containing a wide variety of motifs and fillings.

Mauchline in south-west Scotland, a thriving industry manufactured a wide range of small wooden items, including shuttles, for sale as souvenirs at fashionable resorts. Mauchline-ware shuttles are mostly of sycamore wood with decoration in a variety of finishes, notably tartan and black transfer views.

Tatting pins, attached by a short chain to a metal or bone ring, were used to form picots and make joins. The pins were available in four sizes; the largest, No. 4, was also made in ivory. Instructions were given in *Treasures in Needlework* (1855): 'The pin is used for making an ornamental edge...thus: slip the ring on the left-hand thumb, that the pin attached may be ready for use. After making the required number of double stitches, twist the pin in the circle of cotton, and hold it between the forefinger and thumb whilst making more double stitches; repeat. The little loops thus formed are called picots.'

The pins were not universally popular. The chains got in the way and many workers preferred

Tatting shuttles: (left to right) wood, tortoiseshell, mother-of-pearl, bone; (bottom) crudely carved fruit wood. These are typical of the shuttles widely used in the nineteenth and early twentieth centuries. Prices in 1870 were from 6d to 2s 6d.

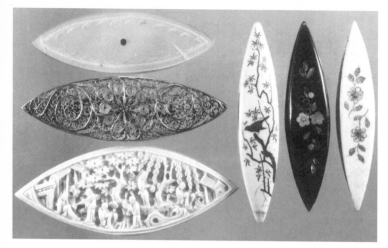

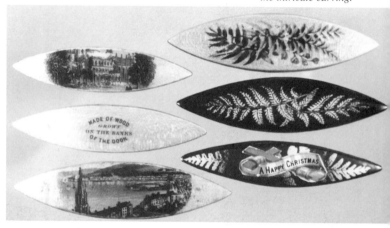

an ordinary large pin. The practice of using a pin was mostly discontinued by the beginning of the twentieth century and the small loop of thread forming the picot was judged by eye.

Tatting required thread which was smooth, strong and firmly twisted. In the eighteenth century Mrs Delany had found that cotton was not strong enough for knotting, but in 1835 John Mercer discovered a way of treating cotton with caustic soda which gave it greater strength and a smoother finish. Known as mercerised thread, it proved to be particularly suitable for tatting. Thread manufactured by Walter Evans & Company of Derby, awarded a medal at the 1862 London Exhibition, was widely recommended. Mrs Pullan described it as strong enough to

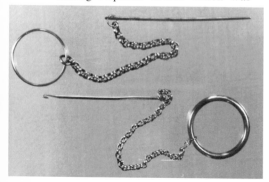

Tatting pins. Contemporary engravings of both pins and hooks are almost invariably labelled 'pins'.

Left: *A rare Tunbridge-ware tatting box, 4 inches (102 mm) long and 2¹/₄ inches (57 mm) wide. It is lined with a blue patterned paper but has no fittings. Most boxes with mosaic inscriptions came from the workshops of Henry Hollamby and Boyce Brown & Kemp but as they were producing this type of design over a long period precise dating is not possible. There appears to be no record of tatting shuttles in Tunbridge ware at that time. More recently they have been produced in small numbers by one or two craftsmen using traditional methods.*

Left: *Design from Mrs Beeton's 'Book of Needlework' (1870) for a circular anti-macassar. 'The illustration shows the fourth of the antimacassar and the whole of the rosette that forms the centre.'*

Below: *The 'Denmark Antimacassar' from Mlle Riego's 'The Royal Tatting Book' (1864). The rosettes are worked in raised tatting, a technique of layering rings.*

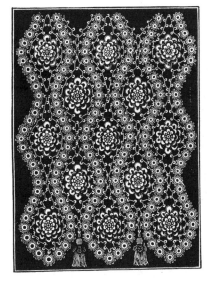

'bear the peculiar jerk necessary to form the knot'. Thread was sold on reels rather than wound into balls. Although surviving pieces of tatting from this period are mostly white, ecru or more rarely black, both Mlle Riego and Mlle Dillmont suggested the use of strong colour, including garnet red, scabious violet and indigo blue. Small tatting workboxes or cases could be purchased. In *The Simple Book of Tat-*

17

Above: *Design for a mantle trimming from 'The Royal Tatting Book' by Mlle Riego (1864). The pattern instructions recommended 'Black Maltese silk for the tatting and sewing silk for the tassels; small jet or steel beads; tatting pin no. 2 and an ivory shuttle'.*

Above: *Fashion plate (detail) from the 'Englishwoman's Domestic Magazine' (October 1864) illustrating 'the newest fashions for autumn and winter mantles'. The trimming round the lower edge of the mantle shows how Mlle Riego's design would have been used. That the tatting pattern and fashion plate were published in the same year indicates that Mlle Riego was producing designs for contemporary fashion.*

Above: *Lace cap from Mrs Beeton's 'Book of Needlework' (1870). 'This very pretty cap consists of an oval crown in tatting, edged all round with a tatted lace; the lappets are made in tatting also. The cap is trimmed with large and small rosettes of narrow blue velvet. A narrow velvet ribbon is drawn through the straight openwork edge of the lace.'*

Right: *Border for the lace cap shown above.*

ting (1867), Mlle Riego advertised a leather tatting case, priced 12s 6d, designed to hold 'Book of Instructions, Cottons and every requisite for the work'. Many tatting containers would have been home-made. Mrs Beeton gave instructions for two small linen bags trimmed with tatting. The York Castle Museum has a tiny case made of blue and green striped and spotted silk ribbon, just large enough to hold a bone shuttle, 'presented by the Misses Pritt of York'.

Ways in which tatting was used often reflected contemporary custom and

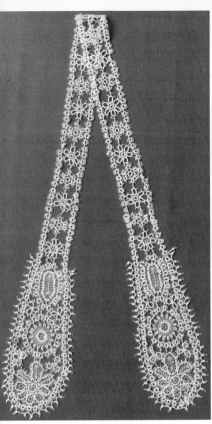

Above left: *Cravat or lappets with extensive use of needlelace centres.*
Above right: *Early Victorian parasol: cream tatted cover over ivory silk.*

fashion. A number of Mlle Riego's books contained an advertisement for Rowlands' macassar hair oil. The oil left marks on

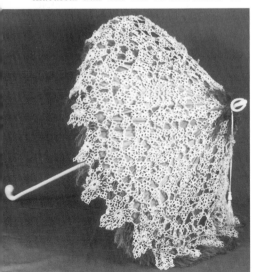

Parasol: cream tatted cover over bright peacock-blue silk.

the backs of chairs unless they were protected by small covers called antimacassars, essential features of a Victorian parlour. Mrs Beeton included a circular design for an elaborate antimacassar, a section of which was illustrated on a fold-out sheet.

Many edgings were intended to trim mantles, cloaks, morning dresses and bonnets. Reviewing the new season's fashions for April 1867 in *The Ladies' Book of the Month*, Madame Elise described 'sleeves of the bishop shape, and waistbands of the same material, edged top and bottom with cluny or tatting, as also the rounded ends which form the sash at the back'. (Cluny was a heavy bobbin lace.)

Collars, cuffs and dress fronts have

Above: *Child's dress from the Rachel B. Kay-Shuttleworth Collections, 1870, with tatted bands.*

Right: *Late nineteenth- or early twentieth-century collar (detail). The thread used is heavier than earlier pieces. The straight inner edge is crocheted, a common feature of nineteenth-century tatting which died out at the beginning of the twentieth century.*

mostly been separated from their garments, but a number of parasols have survived in original, if frail condition. The tatted covers are usually very fine, over a single or double silk lining; the handles, often jointed, are of wood or ivory. The Victoria and Albert Museum, for example, has a parasol with a brown and cream cover over two layers of ivory silk. A pattern for a parasol cover appeared in Mlle Riego's *The Lace Tatting Book* (1866).

Much of the nineteenth-century tatting which has survived is worked in very fine thread, although the quality of workmanship varies. After Mlle Riego, there was little design or technical development, and by the end of the Victorian era the fashion for heavier laces led to increased use of thicker thread.

20

TATTING IN IRELAND

Throughout the Victorian era, tatting was enjoyed as a genteel pastime, mostly without the constraints and challenges of the commercial world. However, in the late 1840s an attempt was made to organise the making and selling of tatting, with other laces, to provide some measure of famine relief in Ireland following the failure of the potato harvest.

Tatting was introduced into the town of Ardee, in County Louth, by Miss Sophie Ellis, one of the daughters of the local rector. She began with two reels of ordinary sewing thread and a shuttle. Her first pupils were a few children, but the skill was soon learned by many of the local women. The designs were based on the familiar circular motif in varying arrangements. Although tatting never assumed the importance of other laces in the Irish lace industry, it had the advantage that in skilled hands it could be made quickly and so sold at a moderate price.

The venture had some success. The tatting of Ardee was exhibited at the Great Exhibition of 1851 and the Dublin Exhibition of 1853. After a few years Miss Ellis was able to distribute £5000 from the sale of tatting. Towards the end of the century it was still creating some employment for the needy, and the Poor Law Guardians acknowledged that but for tatting 'great would have been the increase of the poor depending on the rates for subsistence'. Irish tatting was worked in very fine thread, but the quality of work was not consistent, and designs were repetitive, with little regard for changing taste or fashion. The Ladies Industrial Society, formed in 1847, promoted the sale of Irish laces, with some professional assistance, but the organisation remained mostly with philanthropic amateurs who lacked the expertise to secure a lasting commercial base.

As a result of concern expressed by Irish members of Parliament, a committee was set up in 1884, under Alan S. Cole of the Department of Science and Art in South Kensington, to consider ways

Border of tatting, made at Ardee, County Louth, Ireland, 1880, from the Victoria and Albert Museum.

of reviving the lace industry. It recommended that new designs be commissioned from schools of art and distributed to the lace workers of Ireland. By the end of the century Irish lace could be purchased in big stores in London, France and the United States of America, but tatting did not repeat its early success.

1900 TO 1945

An outstanding contribution to the craft came in 1910 with the publication of *The Art of Tatting* by Lady Katharin Hoare, containing illustrations of tatting by Lady Katharin and Queen Elizabeth of Romania. The designs were remarkable in their innovative use of freestyle forms, metallic and coloured threads and semi-precious stones. Much of Queen Elizabeth's work was ecclesiastical and included a chalice cover in very fine white silk with pearls. The silk thread was drawn through the pearls with a hair and then tatted into the work. Queen Elizabeth is believed to have given her tatting to the monastery of Sinaia in the Carpathians to prevent the jewels falling into the hands of her husband's mistress.

Lady Katharin made extensive use of the chain as a design element. Her enthusiastic use of two shuttles, which allowed the threads to be interchangeable, was typical of her creative approach. Her finest work is of trailing sprays of roses, lilies, clusters of grapes, vine leaves with tendrils, acorns and pomegranates, mostly mounted on fine Brussels net. Had *The Art of Tatting* included working instructions, it might have been a major influence on contemporary design and technique.

Needlework magazines and women's periodicals, such as *Fancy Needlework Illustrated* and *The Lady's World*, were the main source of patterns at the beginning of the twentieth century. Many of the designs retained a strong Victorian influence. Instructions with mistakes and ambiguities were not uncommon. Designs were frequently constructed of many small motifs. A tablecloth in *Girls Own*, about the time of the First World War, contained over nine hundred basic six-ring motifs to be arranged round 144 pieces of linen. Few completed pieces of this complexity have ever been found, and it is doubtful if many of them were actually worked, other than by the original designers.

A number of nineteenth-century designs

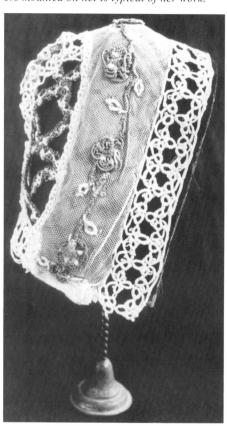

A bonnet by Lady Katharin Hoare from the Rachel B. Kay-Shuttleworth Collections tatted in cream, purple and gold threads. The trailing floral spray with raised flowers mounted on net is typical of her work.

had been named after traditional laces, such as Venetian and Chantilly, and the practice continued into the twentieth century. A design described as 'Tatted Honiton Lace' appeared in an early *Butterick Fashion Guide*, but tatting could never closely imitate or copy fine bobbin laces.

Tatting was sometimes combined with novelty braids or cords, some of which were imported from Germany. In a variety

Child's bib worked from Weldon's 'Practical Teneriffe Lace and Irish Tatting' (1902). The instructions suggested ribbon ties and a plain linen or silk lining. The pattern is typical of the period: an all-over design of trefoils and stars which by judicious arrangement could be used for a variety of purposes – 'for the front of a lady's vest between revers, for a collarette and cuffs, or for a handkerchief or for a pincushion top, square d'oyley, or looking glass cloth'.

of designs and up to about ¹/₂ inch (12 mm) wide, they were usually edged with picots to which the tatting or crochet could be joined during working. One of the plainest was the 'Coronation Cord', a rolled padded cord alternately thick and thin. A more elaborate braid alternated a firm narrow cord with openwork imitating bobbin lace. 'Cotton Picot Vandyke' resembled modern ricrac braid. Patterns of the period promoted their use as giving variety to design and allowing the work to progress more quickly than if entirely of tatting.

A lace sample book from India, dating from before the First World War, indicates that some tatting was being made commercially. The samples include four very simple but neatly worked tatted edgings with straight crochet chain footings. Each sample has a reference number, and prices per yard for a 25 yard length were from threepence to sixpence. There was a 10 per cent discount for the local merchant from whom the ladies of the Raj would have ordered their trimmings. The wholesalers were Rylands & Sons of England. The lace may have been imported from England but it is more likely to have been made in India.

By the 1920s there was a vogue for tatted lingerie, particularly camisoles and boudoir caps. Again, instructions were often inadequate. A camisole in *Crocheted and Tatted Yokes and Neckwear* (1918) by Mary E. Fitch was worked entirely in tatted wheels, reminiscent of early Victorian design. Instructions were given for the wheel, but shaping and overall design had to be guessed from the illustration.

From the 1930s thread manufacturers, such as the Spool Cotton Company in the United States, published a range of pattern booklets

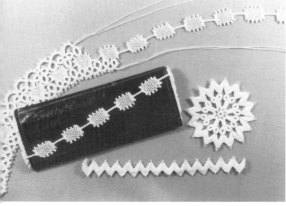

Decorative braids could be purchased to combine with tatting.

Early twentieth-century camisole. The ribbon insertion was both decorative and practical. In 1925 a correspondent to 'Needlecraft' magazine complained that her tatted shoulder straps stretched to nearly twice their original length. She was advised to back them with ribbon.

to promote their products. Designs were mainly smaller collars, trimmings and mats in a wide variety of shapes and sizes. The patterns were more accurate, the older terminology replaced by clear but lengthy instructions. Popular makes of thread, then sold almost universally in balls, included Ardern and Coats.

Popular brands of crochet thread which were available in the early twentieth century: Ardern, Chadwick, Coats & Clark. Some included 'tatting' in advertising and on ball bands.

Sterling silver shuttles, early twentieth century.

American advertising shuttle, beige celluloid. 'YOURS FOR HEALTH Lydia E. Pinkham's VEGETABLE COMPOUND' is printed on the reverse. Lydia Pinkham (1819-83) claimed her patent medicine could cure any 'female complaint'. In 1879 her son Daniel began to use his mother's portrait to advertise the home-made quality of the compound. The shuttle probably dates from around 1900.

Plain bone shuttles, often handed down, appear to have been widely used. Shuttles with an integral hook or pick became popular in the USA.

Some tatting continued during the Second World War, probably because it was a craft which required little in terms of resources or space.

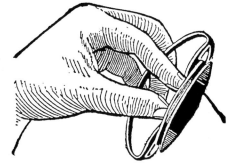

An American advertisement in 1917 for the 'Ideal' tatting shuttle holder, 'the only practical device for winding a tatting shuttle'.

Dorset Feather Stitchery edged with tatting.

MODERN DEVELOPMENTS

In the 1940s and 1950s tatting was often combined with embroidery. In *Every Woman's Complete Guide to Tatting*, published in Australia in the late 1940s, Norma Benporath included a number of patterns for household linen incorporating tatting of traditional technique and design with embroidered floral sprays and cutwork, which she described as complementing without detracting. The book was notable for the size and complexity of some of the projects. Norma Benporath's work was photographed in an elegant 1940s setting, on dark polished furniture and silver trays, with afternoon teacloths and dressing-table sets under fine crystal and china.

A few years later Olivia Pass used tatting effectively to edge some of the aprons and mats embroidered with Dorset Feather Stitchery, a form of embroidery she evolved with members of the Dorset Women's Institutes from motifs found on nineteenth-century smocks and eastern European work. The tatting was usually a close design in a thread of medium thickness, worked in white and then dyed to tone with the embroidery.

About the same time, a new selection of pattern books was published by the thread manufacturers J. & P. Coats, and by William Briggs under the tradename 'Penelope'. Instructions were detailed and reliable. The designers employed by the companies remain anonymous as no records were kept. Designs were similar to those of the previous decades but the tatting was given a completely new look by being photographed in contemporary surroundings – the clean lines and abstract shapes of 1950s furniture and furnishings, some of which were supplied by Peter Jones of Sloane Square, London. The Victorian antimacassar had become the twentieth-century chairback; the elegant collars of an earlier age had given way to smaller neater designs. Patterns for fashion accessories were popular.

J. & P. Coats were the major suppliers of good-quality crochet cotton in a range of colours and thicknesses. Brightly coloured plastic shuttles proved to be extremely hard-wearing and pleasant to use.

A New Look in Tatting (1959) was the first of three innovative books by Elgiva Nicholls. A Fellow of the Society of Designer Craftsmen, she fully explored every facet of the craft. Elgiva Nicholls encouraged creativity based on a firm foundation of technical expertise; in her hands

Gloves with tatted backs from 'Tatting for Dress and Home' (J. & P. Coats, late 1950s). The gloves were worked in No. 60 ecru crochet cotton, pinned on to the backs of navy-blue fabric gloves, the fabric cut away and the tatting sewn on to the glove fronts. The wrist band is crocheted.

tatting became an art form. She described her freestyle forms, mostly of wild flowers and leaves, as drawing with the shuttle, and working in colour, blending and contrasting tones and shades, as painting with the shuttle. Motifs were mounted on paper or fabric as bouquets, sprays or growing plants. Her patterns, which included the thistle, honeysuckle, wild rose and blackberry, emphasised the principle of construction which the worker could modify, rather than prescriptive instructions. She explored the use of multiple threads and exploited the picot, sometimes cutting and fraying it to give a petal a more solid appearance. While researching tatting forms, Elgiva Nicholls studied tatting from Europe and visited the United States. Her experimental work was seen in the USA, Mexico, Rhodesia, New Zealand and Australia. She died in 1982 at the age of eighty-two.

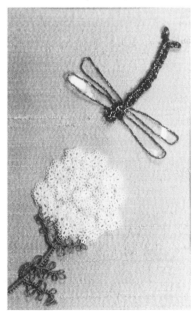

The author's interpretation of a detail from Elgiva Nicholls's design 'Queen Anne's Lace and Dragonfly' ('Tatting', 1962). Elgiva Nicholls gave a detailed description of her methods but did not include precise pattern instructions: 'Work three or four doubles'; 'Continue with the chain as long as necessary'. The end of the stalk is concealed under the edge of the flower and not joined to it. The dragonfly is worked with double metallic thread; the wings are very large picots, filled with cellophane slightly crumpled to catch the light.

27

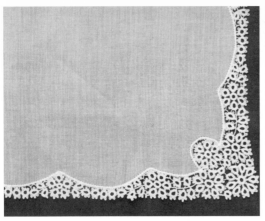

Purchased in Liberty of Regent Street in the 1980s, this is one of three handkerchiefs simulating tatting which were manufactured by Lehner of Switzerland. Of the other two, one had a corner only and the other was a more elaborate design. Usually referred to as 'chemical lace', the tatting is actually machine embroidery on synthetic gauze which is dissolved by chemicals, leaving the embroidery to resemble lace. Chemical lace was first introduced in the 1880s.

A modern maker of shuttles, A. P. Kingston, works mainly in yew, using only timber from storm damage or necessary tree surgery. The wood is dried for two years before use. Partly made shuttles are on the bench, some in 'G' cramps to secure the components together.

Tatting made in China is sold in many tourist areas; similar pieces have been purchased in places as far apart as Hong Kong, Cyprus and California. There is little variety in design. The inclusion of crochet is a typical feature. The pattern almost certainly originated in Europe and would have been taken to China by missionaries.

Peacock, designed and worked by the author using mostly traditional techniques. The three rings forming the crest are Josephine rings; the neck is pearl tatting, a double-sided chain requiring two ball threads.

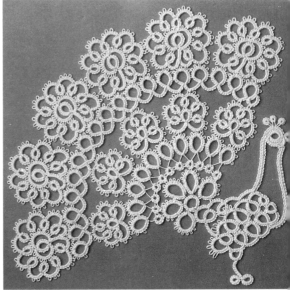

Late twentieth-century crafted shuttles: (left) carved bone, Tunbridge 'tumbling blocks', scrimshaw on horn; (right) hand-painted pansy on boxwood, yew, Tunbridge mosaic, kingwood with decorative wood inlay. The last shuttle is made from a solid piece of wood with two narrow slits which allow the thread to be wound in the centre.

Until recently there was very little structured teaching of tatting. The basic technique had been handed on and tatters, in the main, were content to work familiar easy patterns. But in the 1970s interest revived in the whole range of lace crafts and classes on the techniques of tatting began to become available. With this revival came new designs incorporating almost forgotten techniques. Instructions are now more concise, making use of symbols and diagrams. A small number of craftsmen are producing attractive shuttles. Tatters of the new generation are more adventurous in their choice of yarns and look for new ways to develop and use tatting.

Above: *Collar designed and worked by Heather Lickley, 1990. Traditional edgings in a variety of thick random dyed cotton in greens, mauves and cream incorporate rainbow mixed beads and bugles of glass, wood and plastic. The shuttle used was large enough to hold sufficient thread to complete each row.*

Right: *A unique shuttle, crafted in silver from a tatted motif. Details of the 'stitches' can be clearly seen. Approximately 2³/4 inches (70 mm) long, the shuttle is completely functional and was made in 1986 by Frank Newborn for his daughter, who tatted the original motif.*

DIRECTIONS FOR TATTING

Tatting has a reputation of being difficult to learn from a book, but the following instructions for tatting rings from *An Elementary Course in Tatting* (J. & P. Coats, 1940s) may encourage the reader to try this delightful and – once mastered – relaxing craft. Beginning with a thread no finer than No. 20, wind mercerised crochet cotton on to the shuttle.

Tatting terminology has never been standardised. The following are examples of terms which have been used for the three main components of tatting: *ring*: loop, oval, eyelet, oeillet; *chain*: double thread, reel thread, work a bar, straight thread, scallop; *picot*: purl, pearl, pinstitch, double loop stitch.

Position of thread

Left hand

Hold the thread about 3 inches (75 mm) from the end between the first finger and the thumb. Wind it round the first, second and third fingers at the first joints and up again to the first finger and thumb, where it is held fast (figure 1). Leave sufficient space between the first and second finger to allow the shuttle to pass backwards and forwards.

Right hand

Hold the shuttle loosely between the first finger and thumb. Pass the thread over the second and third finger and round the little finger (figure 1).

Method

Under knot or single stitch

Pass the shuttle under 'A' and 'B', slipping 'B' between the first finger of the right hand and the shuttle. Bring back the shuttle without turning it, over 'B' and under 'A'; drop the second finger of the left hand (figure 2). Pull the shuttle tight (figure 3). Lift up 'B' with the second finger of the left hand and gradually work the knot along towards the left thumb, keeping the shuttle-thread tight all the time.

It is when tightening the knot that the difficulty arises, as 'A', the shuttle-thread, is originally knotted on to 'B' and it is in slackening 'B' and tightening 'A' that the knot is converted on to 'A'. Unless the knot is formed on the shuttle-thread it will not draw up.

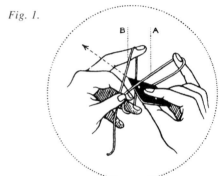

Fig. 1.

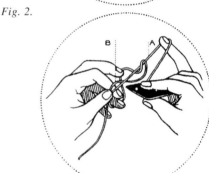

Fig. 2.

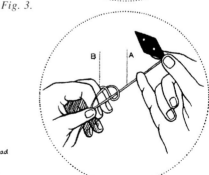

Fig. 3.

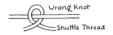

Wrong Knot

Shuttle Thread

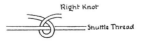

Right Knot

Shuttle Thread

Over knot or double stitch
    Start with both hands in the same position (figure 1) but drop the thread off the little finger of the right hand. Pass the shuttle over 'B' between the thumb and the shuttle, then back again, slipping 'B' between the first finger and the shuttle and through the loop of loose shuttle-thread (figure 4). Tighten and draw up the thread in the same way as the under knot.

Fig. 4.

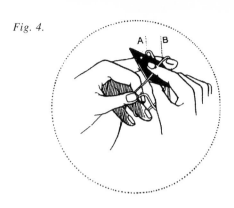

This completes the double stitch (ds). Keeping the thread round the left hand, work eight or nine more double stitches. Gently pull the shuttle thread to close the ring. This ring should be practised until it can be worked with confidence. Figures 5-7 show how to introduce and join picots. When a picot (p) has been formed the next double stitch will already have been tatted.

Fig. 5 (top). Fig. 6 (bottom).

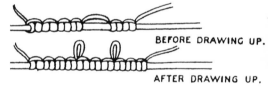

BEFORE DRAWING UP.

AFTER DRAWING UP.

To form a picot
    Leave a space equal to three doubles, then work a double and draw up. A loop is formed (figures 5 and 6), which is the picot.

To join picots
    Take a crochet hook and draw the loop that is round the fingers through the last picot. Pass the shuttle through the loop (figure 7), keeping the shuttle-thread tight. This joining counts the under knot of the next stitch.

Fig. 7.

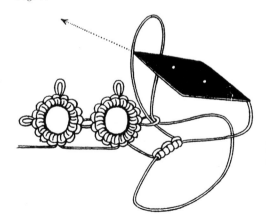

Scallop edging

A simple trimming can be worked by tatting a series of rings similar to those in figure 7. *Double stitch*: ds; *picot*: p.

Ring 1 – 4ds. p. 4ds. p. 4ds. p. 4ds. Close ring. Leave a short length of unworked thread.
    Ring 2 – 4ds. Join to last p. of first ring. 4ds. p. 4ds. p. 4ds. Close ring. Continue for length required.
    This is a favourite edging for handkerchiefs and baby linen. Variations of it can be found in many tatting books including those by Mlle Riego and Mrs Beeton.

FURTHER READING

Hoare, Lady Katharin. *The Art of Tatting*. Batsford, 1988. (Originally published in 1910.)
Jones, Rebecca. *The Complete Book of Tatting*. Dryad Press, 1985.
Konior, Mary. *Tatting in Lace*. Dryad Press, 1988.
Nicholls, Elgiva. *Tatting: Technique and History*. Dover, 1984. (Originally published in 1962.)

Information on shuttles may also be found in publications dealing with antique needlework tools.

PLACES TO VISIT

It is advisable to telephone or write before making a visit. Most collections of tatting are small and unlikely to be on display.

Castle Museum, Norwich, Norfolk NR1 3JU. Telephone: 01603 223624.
Gawthorpe Hall, Padiham, near Burnley, Lancashire BB12 8UA. Telephone: 01282 778511. (The Rachel B. Kay-Shuttleworth Collections.)
Luton Museum and Art Gallery, Wardown Park, Luton, Bedfordshire LU2 7HA. Telephone: 01582 746723.
National Museum of Ireland, Kildare Street, Dublin 2, Republic of Ireland. Telephone: 01 661 8811.
Victoria and Albert Museum, Cromwell Road, South Kensington, London SW7 2RL. Telephone 0171-938 8500.
York Castle Museum, Tower Street, York YO1 1RY. Telephone: 01904 653611.

FURTHER INFORMATION

The Ring of Tatters is an association of tatters which encourages the development and promotion of the craft. Enquiries to 269 Oregon Way, Chaddesden, Derbyshire DE21 6UR.